ZOOM!

Dinosaurs

CHERRYTREE BOOKS

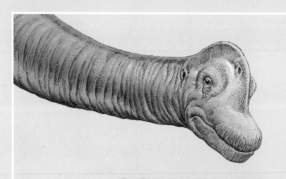

CONTENTS

ZOOM!

Dinosaurs

First published in this edition in 2004 by Cherrytree Books,
a division of Evans Brothers Ltd, 2A Portman Mansions,
Chiltern St, London W1U 6NR

Created and produced by Nicholas Harris and
Claire Aston, Orpheus Books Ltd.

Text Nicholas Harris

Consultant Professor Michael Benton, Department of
Earth Sciences, Bristol University

Illustrated by Inklink, Firenze

ISBN 1 842342 30 4

A CIP record for this book is available from the British
Library.

Printed and bound in Singapore.

LET'S ZOOM!

When you use the zoom feature on a camera, you bring pictures from distance to close-up without moving it. For example, you can capture the image of a butterfly on a leaf while keeping your distance. This book works in exactly the same way.

Imagine you were able to travel back in time 150 million years and point a camera at the whole Earth. The illustration on pages 6 and 7 shows what you would see in your viewfinder (Earth looked very different then). Now zoom in to one part of the scene. You may find yourself looking at a landscape of erupting volcanoes and steaming, swampy forests. There are no signs of cities, roads or farmland, of course, only wild nature. Keep zooming, and you will eventually arrive in the unforgettable world of the most awesome creatures that ever walked on this planet: the dinosaurs. As you zoom in further, you'll witness a titanic contest between a giant, long-necked dinosaur and its terrifying predators. You'll make out much smaller inhabitants of the dinosaur world as they dart through the undergrowth. You'll discover a nest hidden away in that undergrowth, an egg and a tiny dinosaur embryo inside that egg.

It's a fascinating journey, yet you will not have to move one millimetre! And you'll discover some amazing things about dinosaurs that only this incredible *zooming* book can show you . . .

JURASSIC EARTH

About 150 million years ago, during the Jurassic Period, Earth's continents were much closer together than they are today. Only narrow, shallow seas separated Europe, North America and Asia. South America, Africa, Antarctica and Australia were all joined together in a "super-continent" known as Gondwana.

How do continents move? Earth's surface is divided into a number of slabs, called plates. Driven by currents in the molten rock inside Earth, they gradually slide around the globe. Whole continents may drift thousands of kilometres, colliding with others or splitting apart.

ZOOM IN TO EARTH TO VIEW A JURASSIC LANDSCAPE

LANDSCAPE

Just as the shapes of Earth's continents and oceans were very different millions of years ago, so too were Earth's landscapes. Worldwide, the climate was warm and humid, with moist winds from the oceans bringing rain to inland regions.

SHALLOW SEAS COVERED MANY AREAS IN JURASSIC TIMES

With all polar ice melted, sea levels were higher than they are today. Active volcanic eruptions beneath the ocean waters along the cracks in Earth's crust raised the sea floor, making sea levels even higher.

Swampy lowlands covered great tracts of land in Jurassic times. A typical landscape was lush and green.

ZOOM DOWN TO A SWAMP IN THE JURASSIC LANDSCAPE

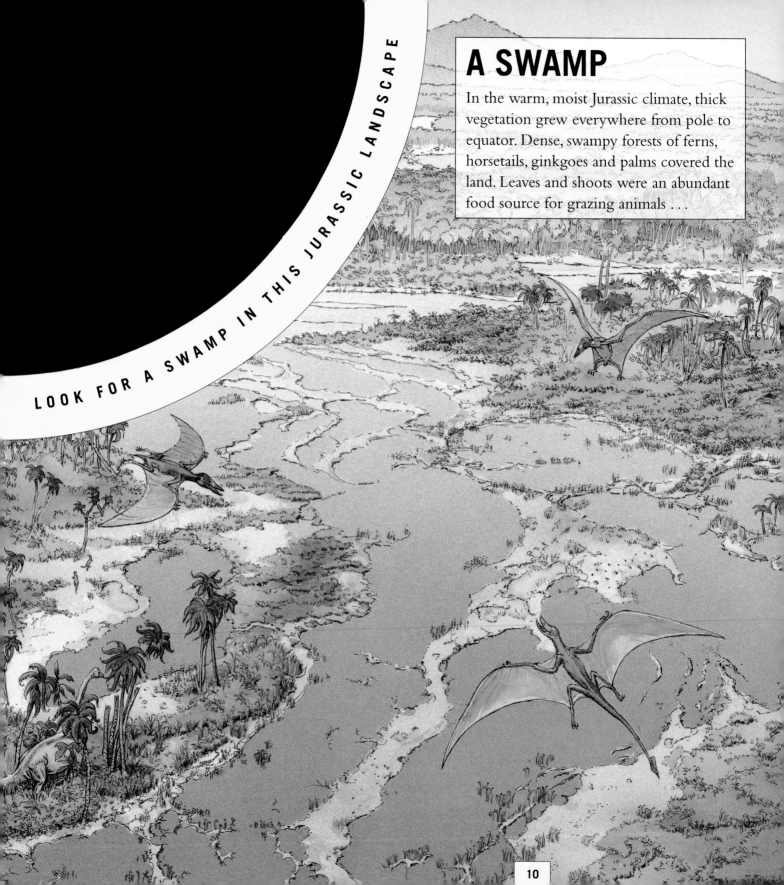

A SWAMP

In the warm, moist Jurassic climate, thick vegetation grew everywhere from pole to equator. Dense, swampy forests of ferns, horsetails, ginkgoes and palms covered the land. Leaves and shoots were an abundant food source for grazing animals . . .

Pterosaurs—flying reptiles—circled above the land, especially near coasts, where fish, their main source of food, were plentiful. Pterosaurs' wings were made of sheets of skin linking their fourth fingers to their bodies. They had toothed beaks, perfect for plucking fish out the water and carrying them away.

ZOOM DOWN TO DISCOVER THE DINOSAURS

DINOSAURS

Some of the largest animals ever to walk on Earth lived during the Jurassic Period. The sauropods *(see page 26)* were a group of plant-eating dinosaurs up to 30 metres in length. Some could bite off leaves from trees 12 metres high. Rearing up on their hind limbs, they could go higher still.

Cetiosaurus

Brachiosaurus

LOOK FOR THE DINOSAURS IN THIS VAST SWAMP

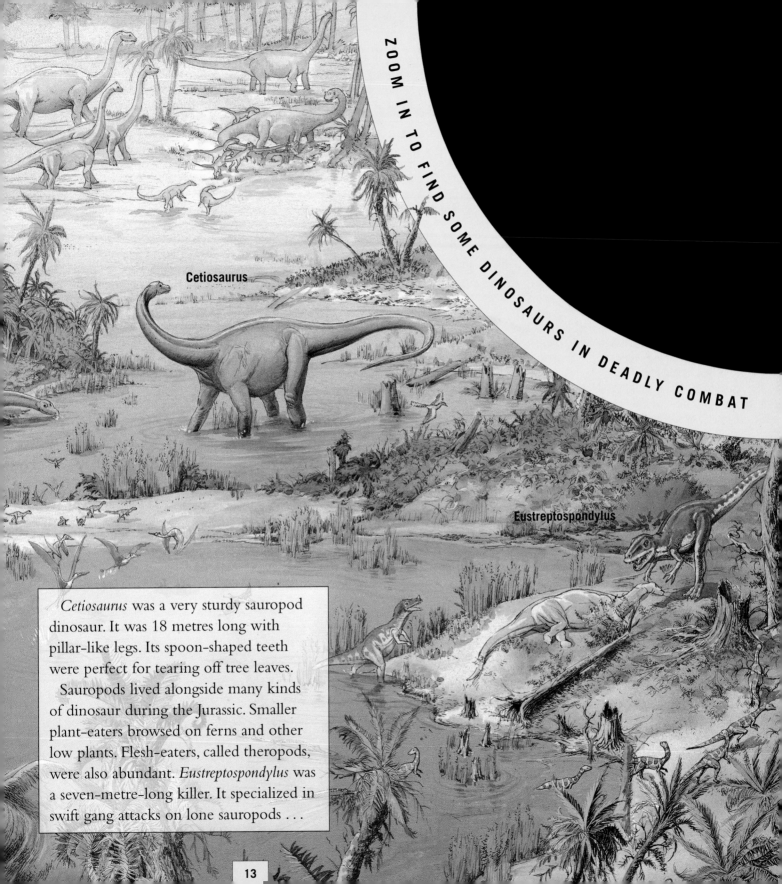

Cetiosaurus

Eustreptospondylus

Cetiosaurus was a very sturdy sauropod dinosaur. It was 18 metres long with pillar-like legs. Its spoon-shaped teeth were perfect for tearing off tree leaves.

Sauropods lived alongside many kinds of dinosaur during the Jurassic. Smaller plant-eaters browsed on ferns and other low plants. Flesh-eaters, called theropods, were also abundant. *Eustreptospondylus* was a seven-metre-long killer. It specialized in swift gang attacks on lone sauropods . . .

ATTACK!

Although they were much smaller dinosaurs, several *Eustreptospondylus* might launch an attack on a massive *Cetiosaurus* together. The predators would circle their chosen victim, watching it very carefully.

For what it lacked in speed, *Cetiosaurus* made up for in sheer size. It could rear up on its back legs and crash down on its attackers. It might also flick its whip-like tail with great force into a predator's face, perhaps inflicting a fatal blow. But if they could avoid *Cetiosaurus*' counter-attack, the *Eustreptospondylus* gang would rush at their prey, using their claws and dagger-like teeth to bring it down.

ZOOM DOWN TO THE GROUND BENEATH THE DINOSAURS' FEET

TINY DINOSAURS

Not all dinosaurs were lumbering giants or powerful killers. Some, like *Compsognathus*, were swift, cat-sized creatures that hunted for lizards, insects or small mammals in the undergrowth. This tiny, slim dinosaur had thin legs and bird-like feet and looked similar to *Archaeopteryx*, one of the earliest-known birds. The two animals actually lived in the same part of the world at the same time, and may have been closely related.

FIND THE TINY DINOSAURS RUSHING ALONG THE GROUND

Compsognathus was quick on its feet. It may have been able to outrun lizards or catch dragonflies in flight.

Archaeopteryx

Compsognathus

Archaeopteryx was about the size of a chicken. Like its probable ancestors, flesh-eating dinosaurs, it had teeth and a long, bony tail. It also had feathers and wings, and could probably fly—or at least glide from tree to tree. *Archaeopteryx* may have fed on insects.

FIND THE NEST HIDDEN AWAY IN THE UNDERGROWTH

DINOSAUR NEST

Here, some baby dinosaurs have hatched, fully formed and already on their feet and in search of food. Like birds, many dinosaurs made nests for their eggs. Some dinosaur mothers stayed by the nest to protect the eggs and the tiny hatchlings. Despite their best efforts, however, the eggs (and the hatchlings) were an easy source of food for small mammals and other dinosaurs.

TAKE A CLOSER LOOK AT WHAT'S INSIDE THE EGGS

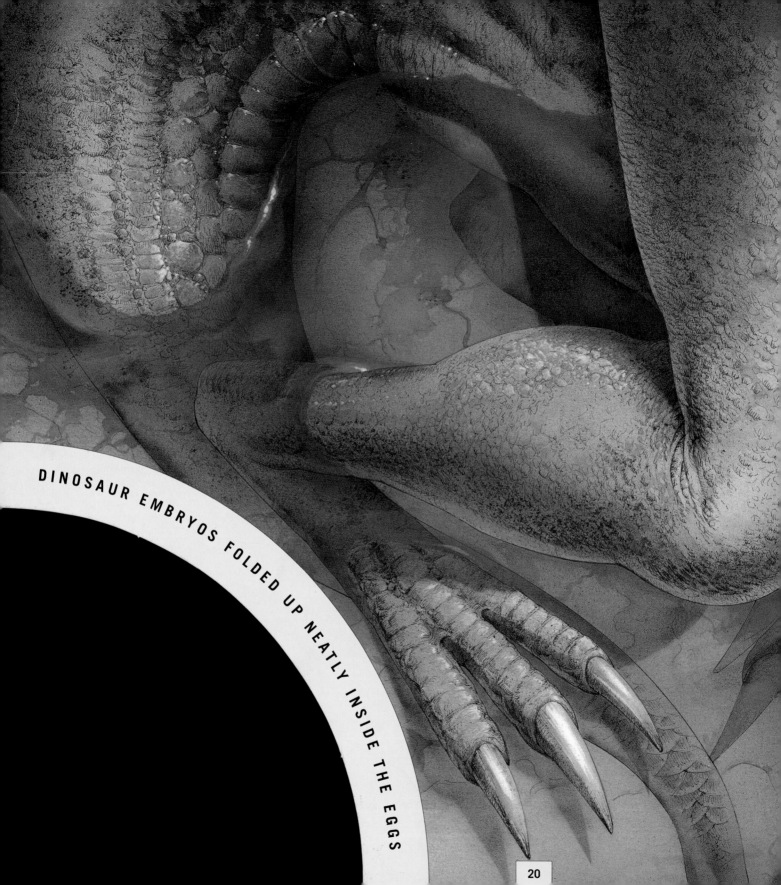

DINOSAUR EMBRYOS FOLDED UP NEATLY INSIDE THE EGGS

INSIDE AN EGG

Dinosaur eggs were hard-shelled with tiny holes in the walls, allowing the baby dinosaurs inside to breathe. When ready to be born, the hatchlings simply knocked the tops off and climbed out. In some kinds of dinosaur, the hatchlings were still not fully developed and so depended on their parents for care. In others, the babies (like this *Megalosaurus*) were born fully formed and able to fend for themselves immediately.

TAKE A CLOSE LOOK AT THE SKIN OF THE BABY DINOSAUR

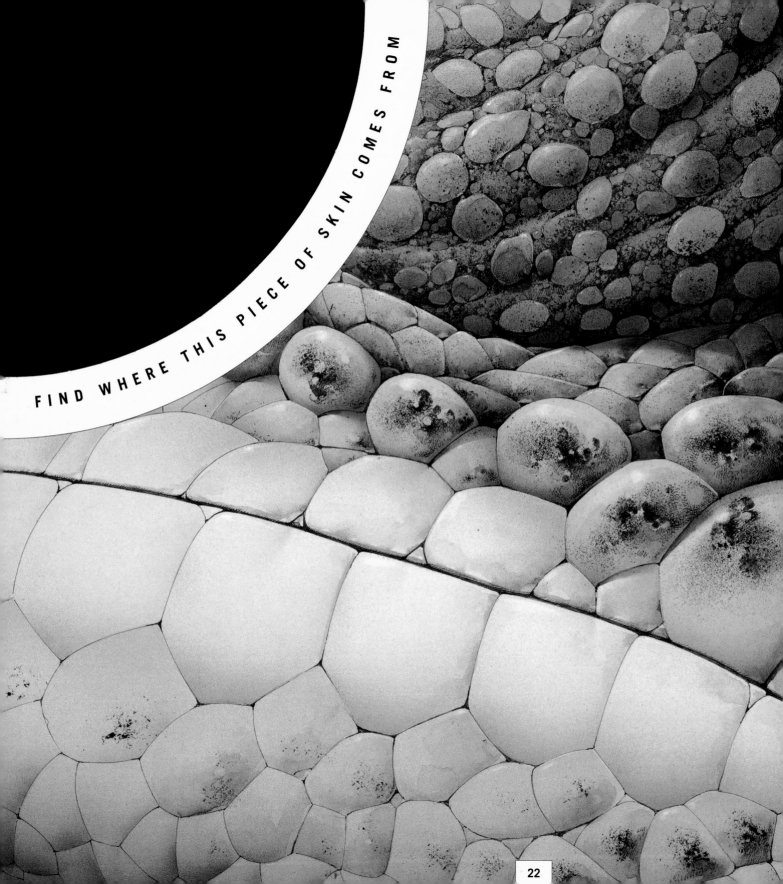

FIND WHERE THIS PIECE OF SKIN COMES FROM

SKIN

Dinosaur skin was quite similar to that of modern reptiles. There were scales of different shapes—some round, some hexagonal. They varied in size according to the part of the body they covered. The scales were not overlapping (as they are on snakes and lizards), but separated from one another by areas of thinner skin.

How can we tell what colours the dinosaurs' skins were? Nobody knows. All we can do is make guesses based on the colours of modern reptiles.

The ancestors of the dinosaurs basked in the swamplands of the Carboniferous forests. Heavy, lumbering amphibians, some more than two metres long, still spent much of their time in the water. Living alongside the giant dragonflies and centipedes was the tiny reptile, Hylonomus.

Dendrerpeton (amphibian)

Hylonomus

ORIGINS

Dinosaurs were reptiles that lived on land 230-65 million years ago, during the Triassic, Jurassic and Cretaceous Periods. Unlike other reptiles, they walked upright on legs held beneath their bodies, like birds and mammals. For more than 160 million years, dinosaurs of many kinds and sizes dominated life on land until they, along with marine and flying reptiles, became extinct (see page 28).

The first reptiles had evolved about 320 million years ago, during the Carboniferous Period. They were descended from **amphibians**, animals with fish-like heads and tails but with four legs instead of fins. In the hot, swampy forests that blanketed the lowlands of Europe and North America at this time, amphibians quickly multiplied.

Dimetrodon *lived during the Permian Period. It was a pelycosaur—not a dinosaur. Its sail may have helped control its body temperature.*

Although capable of living on land, amphibians still kept close to water, where (as frogs and newts do today) they laid their jelly-covered eggs and the young swam like fish. Eventually, some creatures found a way to lay hard-shelled eggs on land, and so became the first **reptiles**.

The tropical forests of the Carboniferous gave way to the dry scrublands of the Permian and Triassic Periods, a development that favoured the reptiles with their ability to lay eggs on land. Reptiles also evolved stronger jaw muscles, enabling them to eat tough desert plants.

Two of the main types included the mammal-like reptiles (from which mammals would later evolve) and the **archosaurs**. Equipped with powerful jaws and bony armour, the archosaurs became dominant during the Triassic Period. Early archosaurs had a sprawling gait, but later in the Triassic, some kinds began to stand more upright. About 230 million years ago, the first dinosaurs, also from the archosaur group, evolved. They were able to run around on their hind legs, leaving their arms free to grasp their prey. Among the early dinosaurs were

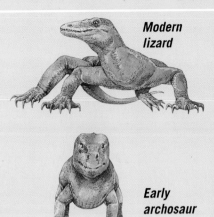
Modern lizard

Early archosaur

Dinosaur

Dinosaurs were land reptiles. Neither marine reptiles nor flying reptiles were dinosaurs, although they lived during the same age. Dinosaurs walked upright, their legs supporting them beneath their bodies, like mammals and birds. This feature is unique to dinosaurs and not seen in other reptiles. Lizards, for example, have sprawling limbs. Some early archosaurs had postures that were halfway between the two.

Coelophysis, fast-moving, three-metre long flesh-eaters that hunted in packs *(below)*. They roamed across what is now the southern United States preying on insects, lizards, small mammals and even other small dinosaurs.

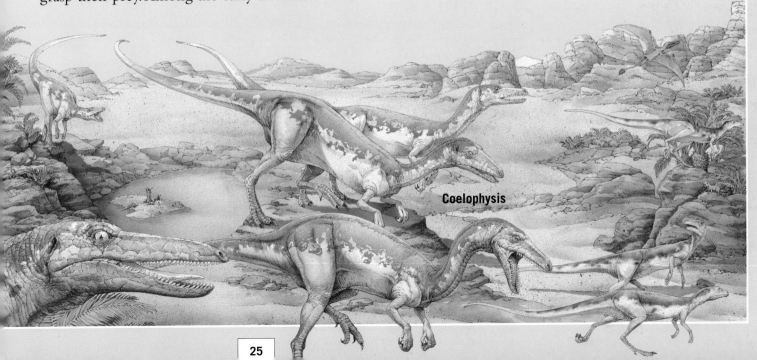
Coelophysis

FAMILIES

There were hundreds of different kinds of dinosaurs. They formed two major groups: the lizard-hips, or **saurischians**, whose hip bones were shaped like those of other reptiles, and the bird-hips, or **ornithischians**, whose hip bones were shaped like those of modern birds. The carnivores (theropods) and the long-necked herbivores (sauropods and prosauropods) were saurischians, while the ornithopod, armoured, plated and horned *(see page 29)* dinosaurs were ornithischians.

The **sauropods** were among the largest animals that ever lived. Some kinds grew to more than 15 metres long. They had small heads, long necks, thick, pillar-like legs and long tails. Moving in herds, the sauropods stripped leaves from the trees with their teeth. If attacked, they might have been able to rear up on their hind legs and bring their weight crashing down on their enemy. Their tails could have been used like whips.

Brachiosaurus, the heaviest dinosaur of all, was a sauropod. The longest dinosaurs were also sauropods: the diplodocids *Apatosaurus, Barosaurus* and *Diplodocus* itself.

The **theropods** (flesh-eaters) varied greatly in size, but most had powerful jaws and sharp teeth. Large theropods, such as *Tyrannosaurus (see page 29)* may have stalked their prey, bringing them down after a short chase. Smaller, swifter carnivores probably hunted in packs.

Plateosaurus (prosauropod)

Brachiosaurus

Stegosaurus

The plated dinosaurs, such as *Stegosaurus,* were large, slow-moving dinosaurs with double rows of bony plates that ran the length of their backs. They also had long spines on their tails, which they may have used to fend off attackers.

Ankylosaurs, the armoured dinosaurs of the Cretaceous Period, were built like tanks. Their massive bodies were encased in thick slabs of bony armour, reinforced by studs and spikes. Only if somehow turned over, exposing their soft underbellies, would they become vulnerable.

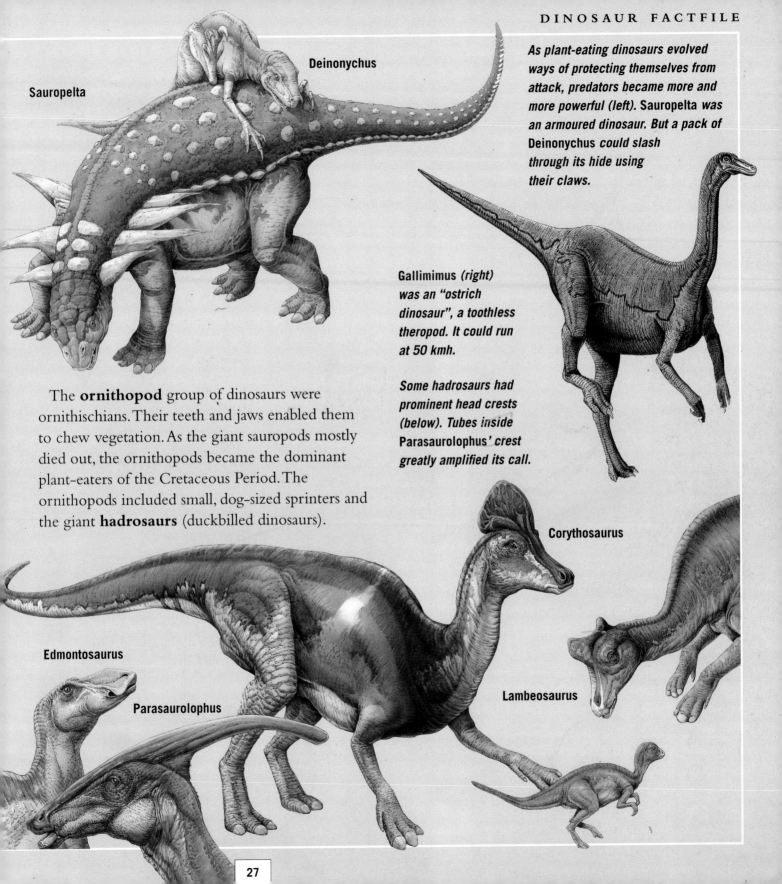

Deinonychus

Sauropelta

As plant-eating dinosaurs evolved ways of protecting themselves from attack, predators became more and more powerful (left). Sauropelta was an armoured dinosaur. But a pack of Deinonychus could slash through its hide using their claws.

Gallimimus (right) was an "ostrich dinosaur", a toothless theropod. It could run at 50 kmh.

Some hadrosaurs had prominent head crests (below). Tubes inside Parasaurolophus' crest greatly amplified its call.

The **ornithopod** group of dinosaurs were ornithischians. Their teeth and jaws enabled them to chew vegetation. As the giant sauropods mostly died out, the ornithopods became the dominant plant-eaters of the Cretaceous Period. The ornithopods included small, dog-sized sprinters and the giant **hadrosaurs** (duckbilled dinosaurs).

Corythosaurus

Edmontosaurus

Parasaurolophus

Lambeosaurus

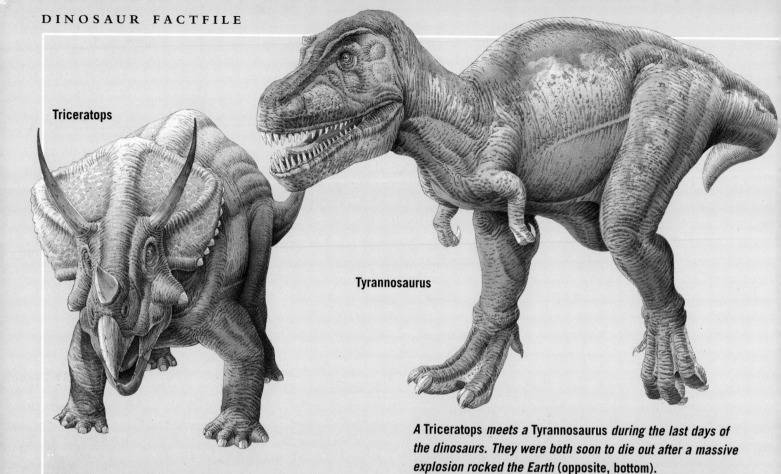

Triceratops

Tyrannosaurus

A Triceratops meets a Tyrannosaurus during the last days of the dinosaurs. They were both soon to die out after a massive explosion rocked the Earth (opposite, bottom).

EXTINCTION

By the end of the Cretaceous Period, about 65 million years ago, all the dinosaurs were extinct. They had ruled Earth for more than 160 million years (by comparison, modern humans have existed for just 150,000 years). No one knows what happened, but the evidence shows that the event was quite abrupt. Many scientists think that a massive **asteroid**—a large rocky object in space— may have crashed into Earth *(right, above)*, punching a large crater and throwing up huge quantities of pulverized rock high into the atmosphere. The sun would have been blotted out, lowering temperatures for years on end. Another theory is that a massive **volcanic eruption** *(right, below)* could have produced the same effect.

Evidence for both theories comes from the discovery by geologists of a layer of metal, called iridium, in late Cretaceous rocks. Iridium is believed to be present only in Earth's core and in asteroids. Iridium dust thrown up by an exploding asteroid or lava from inside Earth may have settled on the surface, then later compacted in the rocks of the time.

The last years of the dinosaurs produced some of the most spectacular kinds. They included the nine-metre giant *Triceratops*, a horned dinosaur with a huge skull and massive bony neck frill, three horns and a parrot-like beak. This plant-eater's defences would have been tested to the full in confrontations with *Tyrannosaurus*, a massive theropod with a huge head and powerful back legs.

But no dinosaur, dependent as they were on warmth and a plentiful supply of food, could survive life in a cold, bleak desert.

While the dinosaurs, along with marine and flying reptiles, perished at the end of the Cretaceous Period, other reptiles, including lizards, snakes and crocodiles, survived. Mammals, at that time all tiny, shrew-like animals, also lived on. With the dinosaurs extinct, they would evolve into a wide variety of families. Birds, the dinosaurs' only descendants, were other survivors. Some took the place of large dinosaurs and evolved into massive predators (right), preying on early kinds of horses!

GLOSSARY

Amphibians Animals that live much of their lives on land, but which have to return to water to breed.

Ankylosaurs Ornithischian dinosaurs fully covered in armoured plates, studs and spikes. Some, for example, *Euoplocephalus,* had tail clubs.

Archosaurs A group of reptiles that first appeared in the late Permian Period and gave rise to the crocodiles, pterosaurs, dinosaurs and birds.

Asteroid A rocky body that orbits the Sun. Asteroids range in size from tiny specks to just under 1000 kilometres in diameter.

Continents The great land masses, such as Asia, Africa and the Americas, that make up the land surface of Earth.

Continental drift The movement of continents around the globe. Earth's outer layer is made up of separate interconnecting pieces, called **tectonic plates**, which are constantly grinding into, away from, or alongside one another, taking continents or parts of continents with them.

Dinosaurs Reptiles that lived on land during the Mesozoic Era (250-65 million years ago) and which walked upright on legs held beneath their bodies, like birds and mammals.

Diplodocids Sauropod dinosaurs with long, slender bodies and tails. They included *Apatosaurus, Seismosaurus* and *Diplodocus*.

Evolution The process by which forms of life have changed over millions of years, gradually adapting to make the best use of their environment.

Hadrosaurs "Duckbilled" dinosaurs from the late Cretaceous Period. Grazing in herds, they were plant-eaters with special grinding teeth.

Horsetails Plants that grew in the great swamp-forests to heights of 15 metres or more. They have regular whorls of spiky branches.

Ornithischians The "bird-hipped" dinosaurs, one of two major types of dinosaur (the others were the saurischians). Ornithischians had backward-slanting pubic bones—the lower part of the hip bone.

Ornithopods Ornithischian dinosaurs that had teeth and jaws enabling them to chew vegetation. The ornithopods ("bird feet") included *Iguanodon, Hypsilophodon* and the hadrosaurs.

Pelycosaurs A group of reptiles, some of which had large sails of skin supported by bone projecting from their backs.

Predators Animals that prey on others.

Prosauropods The first plant-eating dinosaurs, emerging in late Triassic times. Some may have been partly bipedal (moving on two feet).

Pterosaurs Flying reptiles that existed from the late Triassic to late Cretaceous Periods. Their wings were formed from skin flaps between the fourth finger and lower body.

Saurischians The "lizard-hipped" dinosaurs, one of two major types of dinosaur (the others were the ornithischians). Saurischians had forward-jutting pubic bones—the lower part of the hip bone.

Sauropods Long-necked, four-legged, plant-eating dinosaurs. They were the largest and heaviest land animals of all time.

Theropods All the flesh-eating saurischians.

INDEX